THE STATUE

ABRAHAM LINCOLN

A Masterpiece by
Daniel Chester French

THE STATUE

ABRAHAM LINCOLN

A Masterpiece by
Daniel Chester French

Written by *Ernest Goldstein*

Lerner Publications Company • Minneapolis

The publisher wishes to thank Wanda Magdeleine Styka, archivist at Chesterwood, for sharing her expertise throughout the evolution of this project.

Library of Congress Cataloging-in-Publication Data

Goldstein, Ernest, 1933–1996
    The Statue Abraham Lincoln, A Masterpiece by Daniel Chester French / written by Ernest Goldstein.
        p.   cm.
    Includes Index.
    Summary: Describes the thought and effort that went into Daniel French's statue of Abraham Lincoln that is part of the Lincoln Memorial in Washington, D.C., and compares this likeness to others of Lincoln.
    ISBN 0-8225-2067-2 (alk. Paper)
    1. French, Daniel Chester, 1850–1931. Lincoln—Juvenile literature. 2. French, Daniel Chester, 1850–1931—Criticism and interpretation—Juvenile literature. 3. Lincoln Memorial (Washington, D.C.)—Juvenile literature. [1. Lincoln Memorial (Washington, D.C.) 2. French, Daniel Chester, 1850–1931. 3. Statues. 4. National monuments.] I. Title.
NB237.F7A7   1997
730'.92—dc21   96–47607

Manufactured in the United States of America
1 2 3 4 5 6 – JR – 02 01 00 99 98 97

contents

◀ President Abraham Lincoln meets with General George McClellan on the battlefield of Antietam, Maryland, in 1862.

In 1916, an Englishman by the name of Lord Charnwood published a biography of Abraham Lincoln (1809–1865). The book, a success in England, also became a bestseller in the United States. Fifty years after Lincoln's assassination, his fame was still growing.

Fate had been cruel to Mr. Lincoln. He had been president at one of the darkest moments of U.S. history—a time when the nation was in danger of losing not only its soul, but its very existence. Lincoln had been commander in chief during the Civil War (1861–1865), the bloodiest war ever fought. Many of his generals were arrogant and incompetent—no match for the military genius of the Southern Confederacy. His army consisted mainly of untrained volunteers. Even the Union horses from the farms of the Midwest and New England could not do battle with the thoroughbreds of the South.

Abraham Lincoln did not control events as much as he was controlled by them. During his presidency, the conflict within the nation was brutal. In her book *Across Five Aprils,* Newbery Award winner Irene Hunt described the tragedy of the nation through the life of one family in Ohio. The children of that family fought on different sides during the war. Brothers fought brothers; friends fought and killed friends. The country was so divided that whichever way Lincoln turned, whatever decisions he made, he was bound to alienate about half the population. The country needed a savior. And a savior had, indeed, arrived—but he was unannounced. Only when Secretary of War Edwin Stanton announced Lincoln's death with the words, "Now he belongs to the ages," did the nation understand. Only after Lincoln's death was the identity of America's savior revealed.

Fifty years after his assassination, Lincoln was becoming a universal symbol of one country's purpose—a purpose that would give hope to the entire world. It is not surprising, then, that an English lord could write a best-seller about an American president. Charnwood's inspirational style struck home with the American public—especially with Daniel Chester French, a sculptor who lived in Stockbridge, Massachusetts. He obtained a copy

▼ Work begins on the grounds of the Lincoln Memorial.

French modeled this statue of Lincoln standing in front of the Nebraska state capitol.

of Charnwood's book in October 1916. When French read Charnwood's opening statement, "He died with every circumstance of tragedy, yet it is not the accident of his death but the purpose of his life that is remembered," the sculptor was hooked. French's personal notes identify a vision inspired by the book. In June 1920, French wrote to Charnwood that "I have been on my knees to you from the time when I first read your life of Lincoln: the most vivid, the most understanding, and the most just portrayal of him that has ever been written." In *Journey into Fame,* French's daughter Margaret French Cresson quoted

her father: "Great, good common sense, that is what Abraham Lincoln had. It was he who saw straight when all the rest were seeing crooked. He looked upon all things with single vision."

French's statement tells much about him as it does about Lincoln. For years the sculptor's passion had been Lincoln. French had a collection of books, articles, and personal anecdotes about Lincoln. He studied photographs and reproductions of Lincoln. He had even obtained replicas of the Lincoln life mask and hands made by the sculptor Leonard Volk. French had also discussed personal details of Lincoln's life with Robert Lincoln, the president's son.

In 1912 French completed the standing *Lincoln* for the Nebraska legislature. The statue was a commission to celebrate the 100th anniversary of Lincoln's birth. French had worked on this project with the architect Henry Bacon. In the history of American statuary, sculptors and architects often planned their projects jointly.

These two men had been working together for years. They worked on approximately 50 monuments and memorials, including a monument to Henry Wadsworth Longfellow in Cambridge, Massachusetts, and a monument to James Oglethorpe, founder of the Georgia colony, in Savannah, Georgia. In fact, Henry Bacon even designed the sculptor's beautiful home and studio at Chesterwood in Stockbridge, Massachusetts, where it remains as a national museum.

Bacon received the commission to design the Lincoln Memorial on February 1, 1913. Selection of the sculptor was also in the hands of the Lincoln Memorial Commission, but Bacon influenced the choice. He requested that his friend and longtime colleague Daniel Chester French be given the assignment to design the statue that would be placed inside the memorial. Bacon could have chosen a replica of a work by America's most respected sculptor, Augustus Saint-Gaudens (1848–1907).

▲ Architect Henry Bacon designed the structure for the Lincoln Memorial.

◀ Daniel Chester French sculpted the famous Lincoln statue that sits within the memorial.

▶ French's Chesterwood studio, the birthplace of the Lincoln Memorial statue

Saint-Gaudens had developed a worldwide reputation for his simple, naturalistic style. He had created many public monuments, including standing and seated statues of Lincoln for parks in Chicago, Illinois. The British had even put a large replica of one of his Lincoln statues in London's Trafalgar Square.

The idea of a national memorial to Lincoln was first introduced in 1867, two years after Lincoln's assassination, but interest lapsed and was not revived again until 1911, when Congress passed a Lincoln Memorial bill and President William Howard Taft signed it on February 9. President Taft then established the Lincoln Memorial Commission, which chose the site and design of the memorial. Two architects submitted designs to the commission, and Bacon's was chosen.

When Bacon received his commission in 1913, he designed a magnificent Greek temple—a modern Parthenon on the Washington Mall. Few in Congress objected to a Greek temple as a tribute to an American president. It was generally agreed that Greek architecture expressed the ultimate harmony and beauty of natural forces, and many people thought the Parthenon was the greatest masterpiece of Greek sculpture. One of the differences between the basic design of the original Parthenon and Bacon's edifice was the opening on the side instead of at the end of the structure. Bacon turned the building so the sides were at right angles to the Mall. The statue of Lincoln would face the Mall. Bacon wrote in his notes, "The most important object is the statue of Lincoln, which is placed in the center of the Memorial, and by virtue of its imposing position in the place of honor, the gentleness, power, and intelligence of the man,

The design for the Lincoln Memorial, *below,* was based on the Parthenon, *left,* of ancient Greece.

A bronze statue of Abraham Lincoln by Augustus Saint Gaudens stands in Lincoln Park in Chicago, Illinois.

expressed as far as possible by the sculptor's art, predominates."

French was also aware of the importance of the Lincoln statue, but it took him almost two years to even develop a plan for the sculpture that was to be placed inside the memorial. Perhaps part of the sculptor's difficulties with *Lincoln* stemmed from the problem of how to portray a man with so many different roles: the railsplitter, the country lawyer, the shopkeeper, the president, the preserver of the Union, and the Great Emancipator. French

spent the entire summer of 1916 working on a larger-than-life model, but he said he was not satisfied or completely sure of his subject. Then, in October, French secured a copy of Charnwood's biography of Lincoln. It made order out of chaos and gave clarity to the sculptor's vision of Lincoln. Soon after French read the book, he completed the statue. Late in 1916, French wrote to a friend that his aim was "to work from [the] inside outward—to make the spirit of the man the thing and not the exterior." Lord Charnwood's book undoubtedly contributed to this end.

But we cannot hurry our story. For there is a story and much drama involved with the execution and completion of the statue. It was unlike anything the sculptor had ever done before. To this day, millions of people come to Washington, D.C., to gaze at the solitary, brooding *Lincoln*. Viewers are inspired, provoked, even overwhelmed at what they see and feel.

two

When the congressional committee selected Daniel Chester French to sculpt the statue for the Lincoln Memorial, the project should have been his ticket to lasting fame. But it wasn't. This situation is highly unusual since the work is much admired, and popular works are usually linked to the artists who created them. For example, viewers generally link the famous *Mona Lisa* to Leonardo da Vinci, the artist who painted it. Although the Lincoln statue is one of the most recognized in the world, few people know the name Daniel Chester French.

Almost no one associates the statue with its creator, which is not fair to French. He was probably one of the best American sculptors of his time. His statues *The Minute Man* and the standing *Lincoln* appear in art books, but critics have not been kind to him. Perhaps a hidden resentment of the popularity of his work transferred to the artist himself. Art critics tend either to make a passing reference to him or to omit him completely from serious consideration. Although French's *Abraham Lincoln* is a masterpiece, little is known about French himself. This book is one author's attempt to provide a bit of understanding.

The awe-inspiring traits that dazzle the *Lincoln* viewer are hidden in the size, dynamism, and clarity of the sculpture.

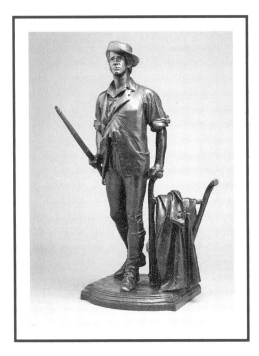

◀ The town of Concord, Massachusetts, awarded French the *Minute Man* commission in 1873.

▼ This period photo shows an early, working model of the statue. The eagle-cornered pedestal was crossed out by French.

Lincoln is seated on a massive chair, with his coat unbuttoned. His face seems lost in contemplation. Such a memorial has inspired noble sentiments and has meant many things to many people. One viewer wrote, "The primary impression is one of rest. The muscles are relaxed, the president is calm, his head high, his torso erect. The body is instilled with life." Another viewer wrote, "There he sits, a majestic figure with the marks of a mighty struggle on his face, and rests a little while. He gazes into the future, thinking of his hopes and plans—so much more for him to do. He must strive on."

These words are noble sentiments, but they have almost nothing to do with the actual statue. The words are not based on visual evidence—on what you see. Often, critics and reviewers respond to a piece of art by revealing feelings from within themselves rather than information about what is actually present. Such personal

◄ Ralph Waldo Emerson, an American essayist and poet

feelings are inspired by the work, but they are primarily subjective and are not necessarily seen or shared by others. The general term for this type of interpretation is called the "intentional fallacy." Intentional fallacy occurs most obviously when viewers and critics delude themselves into thinking they know the ultimate meaning of a work of art, including the intent of the artist.

Art, like life, is too complex for one person to know everything about it. Yet critics and students can be brash enough to imagine that they have found the ultimate meaning. This is a self-deception. Often the artists themselves do not know the meaning of a work of art. When asked,

artists might say something coy—then change their minds and say something else the following day. The serious artist will always try to shy away from the question, "What does your work mean?" Daniel Chester French said that "it is not for the sculptor to tell what the sculpture is about." In a 1922 letter found in *The French Family Papers,* he wrote, "I don't know what to say in answer to your telegram [asking what French meant to express in the Lincoln Memorial statue]. I think it was [Ralph Waldo] Emerson who said that a poet was entitled to credit for anything that anyone finds in his poetry, and I should like to have you interpret what I meant to express by what you find in my statue of Lincoln." In a later letter, regarding another sculpture of his, French wrote, immediately after quoting the same passage from Emerson, "...and surely it is often that an artist puts into his work something that he feels but has never expressed in words."

◀ One of French's clay
working models of *Lincoln*

▶ French thought the statue
had to be in a sitting
position to contrast with
the memorial's vertical
pillars.

The viewer may think that whatever has been said about a work of art has nothing to do with the way he or she feels about it. That belief is acceptable; but it does not go far enough. Appreciation of a work of art depends upon the knowledge the viewer brings to it. Your interpretation is always determined by what you know. So what do you know about the Lincoln Memorial?

Let us begin with the visual evidence and base our conclusions on what we actually see (or what we generally agree everyone sees). For example, as you mount the steps, what do you see first? What is Lincoln doing? He is sitting. (Everyone agrees.) On what? On a chair. What kind of chair? The chair is not like any chair Lincoln really sat on in his lifetime. This chair is based on a design from an ancient Roman chair, which was used by only the highest dignitaries. It provided a symbol of power, dignity, and authority.

Why is Lincoln seated? The answer depends on a knowledge of design and perhaps some art history. French decided to seat Lincoln after Henry Bacon had completed his design of the memorial. Architect and sculptor agreed the site demanded a seated figure because of the vertical columns of the memorial. A standing figure, viewed as another vertical line, would be lost. For "variety and contrast" Lincoln would be seated. Also, a standing figure would place the head too far above the viewer's eye, especially when the viewer got close to the statue. In the final design, note how chair and figure become part of one design. The lines of Lincoln's brow repeat the oval lines of the chair.

What is Lincoln doing while sitting on the chair? Thinking, perhaps brooding. Does he have to be seated in order to think? Obviously not. Look at French's standing *Lincoln* in Nebraska. What do we see? Lincoln is in a standing position, looking down, lost in thought. Just how French decided on Lincoln's position is not clear. A couple of years later, however, the following story was told to French by someone whose mother had seen Lincoln several times on his speaking tours. She had noticed his curious way of standing before he began to speak. He stood with hands clasped in front of him, thinking to himself—in precisely the same pose as French's statue.

Does the position of the Lincoln Memorial statue suggest Auguste Rodin's (1840-1917) sculpture *The Thinker?* Completed in 1888, *The Thinker* is one of the

▲ *The Thinker* by Auguste Rodin

▶ Rodin at work on *The Thinker*

most respected and familiar statues in the world. Its creator is one of the most respected and famous sculptors in the world. Sculptor and sculpture are so closely connected that the sculpture is referred to as "Rodin's *The Thinker.*" The mystery around Rodin is the identity of *The Thinker.* The mystery around the Lincoln sculpture is the identity of the sculptor.

The Thinker resembles no one in particular. He is an everyman. He has the muscles of a brute used to working in the fields or hunting animals. Sitting on a stump, his pose suggests an enormous struggle within himself. Tension is revealed in the enormous muscles of the legs and back. This is not the serene contemplation of a philosopher. This man, with his hand covering his mouth, is shut off from human communication. His downward look accompanies a sideways glance, turned away from people and objects. He has cast the world aside, struggling for the emergence of thought. Many critics have ennobled *The Thinker* with powerful words. For example, one critic wrote that *The Thinker* symbolizes meditation, which, in its terrible effort to embrace the absolute, contracts the athletic body, bends it, crushes it. The brute is struggling to find room in his body for the chain of thought. Another wrote that *The Thinker,* originally titled *The Poet,* represents the creative possibilities inherent in all people.

Why are we spending so much time on Rodin's *Thinker* when this is a book about French's *Lincoln?* Much can be learned from one and applied to the other, because they have a common bond. *The Thinker,*

▶ Leonard Volk made a plaster mask of Lincoln's face.

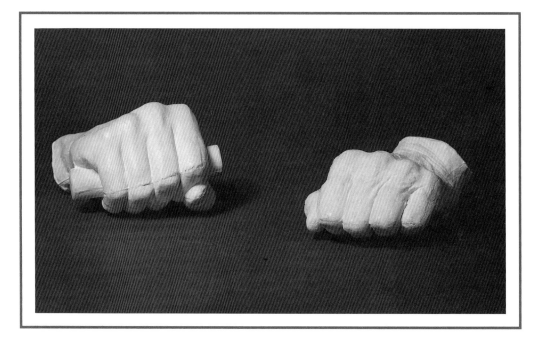

like French's *Abraham Lincoln,* must be considered in terms of the way the artist sculpted him. As you walk around the statue, you get the feeling that every muscle in his body is tensed. What, for example, do the enormous back muscles reveal about *The Thinker?* For good sculpture there is a rule, and for the exceptional sculptor (like Rodin), it is a law: "The human body is a window to the soul." How else, Rodin asks, could a block of stone have the blood and breath of life? The roughly modeled surfaces and compacted composition of *The Thinker* suggest an intense concentration of thought and will.

About the statue in the Lincoln Memorial, French said what he wanted it to show was the strength of the man in his ability to see the job through. Perhaps the hands express this as much as the face. For French, the hands express Lincoln's strength and resolve during conflicts. French undoubtedly spent hundreds of hours studying photographs to achieve the correct portrayal of the hands. In 1922 French wrote, "What I wanted to convey was the mental and physical strength of the great president and his confidence in his ability to carry the thing to a successful finish. If any of this 'gets over,' I think it is probably as much due to the whole pose of the figure and particularly to the action of the hands as to the expression of the face."

In reality, the hands of the *Lincoln* sculpture represent the work of several men.

◀ Leonard Volk's plaster cast
of President Lincoln's hands

▼ Daniel Chester French at
work in his studio at
Chesterwood, his home
in Stockbridge,
Massachusetts

The Portrayal of Hands

Did you ever consider how hands reveal attitudes and emotions? For centuries artists have felt that after the face, the hands and the ears are the keys to the attitude of the subject. One particularly talented art critic was able to identify and authenticate works of art by the way the artist portrayed the hands. This critic suffered a fate worse than that of Daniel Chester French. He lived in near oblivion, but his work goes on. His name is Giovanni Morelli. Morelli identified works of art by examining the hands. Just think how much he had to know, how many paintings he must have studied, to be able to make such conclusions. Hands reveal attitudes. Among the great sculptors, this is a law.

Look at the hands in three pieces of sculpture from perhaps the greatest sculptor who ever lived. Look at them closely and see if you can identify the sculptor. Morelli says that artists repeat the same hands in all their works. But these three pairs of hands are totally different, except in one respect. They are all ideal portrayals of a human hand. Only one artist in the history of

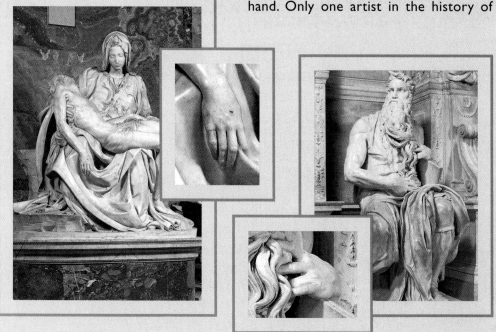

sculpture was capable of making such hands, and that was Michelangelo.

The first hand shown is the right hand of Jesus in Michelangelo's *Pieta*. The arm of the dead Jesus falls gracefully, and his hand delicately catches on a fold in the cloth. Mary is portrayed as a young woman.

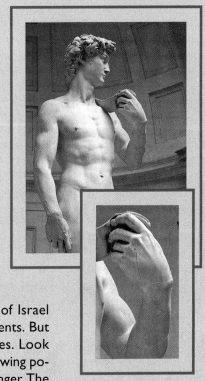

The second set of hands is from Michelangelo's *Moses*. For years it was assumed that Moses was holding the tablets on which the Ten Commandments were written. According to the Old Testament, as Moses rested on his way down the mountain, he saw the children of Israel dancing around a golden calf. Supposedly Moses became so angry that he hurled the tablets down the mountain, because the people of Israel were not worthy of receiving God's commandments. But that is not the way Michelangelo sculpted Moses. Look closer at Moses, at his hands. They are not in a throwing position. Moses's face has a look of surprise and anger. The tablets look as if they might drop out of his right hand. And Moses—caught between surprise and the fear of dropping the words of God—gently, but with enormous strength, holds on to the tablets. Look at the hands and ask yourself what Moses is doing.

The third set of hands is from Michelangelo's *David*. The young David looks like a Greek god, except for those enormous hands. There is no doubt that Michelangelo wants you to see those hands. David is almost ready to use his slingshot. He was skilled in using the slingshot, and his hands played an important role in completing his mission. For centuries, when critics looked at this sculpture, they were filled with admiration for the way Michelangelo portrayed youth. Michelangelo's *David* is immature and not yet fully grown, but he is not a gangling adolescent. He has unnaturally large feet, hands, and head, but he stands alert and watchful—a powerful image of immature strength.

As mentioned earlier, French studied copies of the life casts of Lincoln's hands done by Leonard Volk. According to Volk's published account, he was on a train going to Springfield, Illinois. At a stop along the way, he learned that Lincoln had won the presidential nomination. When Volk arrived in Springfield, he hurried to Lincoln's house, where he was among the first of thousands to shake Lincoln's hand. Volk received permission from Lincoln to make a statue of him. Two days later, the committee appointed by the presidential convention arrived and formally notified Lincoln of his nomination. On the next day, Volk made the casts of Lincoln's hands. Volk suggested that the presidential nominee grasp something in one hand to give variety to the castings. Lincoln disappeared and returned minutes later, whittling off the end of a piece of broom handle. Volk told him that he need not whittle off the edges. "Oh, well," said

Lincoln, "I thought I would like to have it nice."

Notice Lincoln's right hand. It was in this hand that he held the piece of whittled broom stick. Volk's casts show that Lincoln's right hand was considerably swollen, because of the future president's frequent and vigorous handshaking the previous evening. The left hand was bony, however, consistent with Lincoln's lanky frame. During his talk with Volk, Lincoln called attention to a scar at the base of his left thumb, the result of a glancing blow from an ax the year before. This feature is

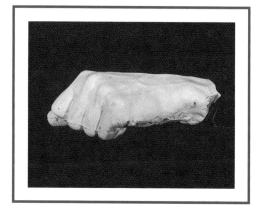

French made many plaster casts of hands before deciding on the final design for the Lincoln Memorial statue. A few examples are shown on this page and the next.

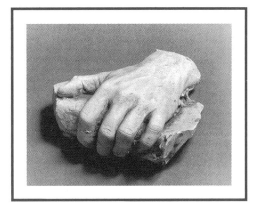

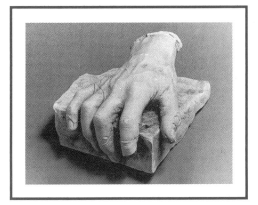

there but almost indistinguishable in French's statue.

The Lincoln hands have been described by many people. One in particular, a provost marshal of the U.S. Army, said, "His hands were more conspicuous even than his feet." An Englishman's impression of Lincoln was "A man six foot high with large, rugged hands which grasped you like a vice when shaking yours." Lincoln's hands may have been shaped by the physical labor of his younger years. Lincoln himself said in a short autobiographical statement written in 1860, "Abraham, the very young, was large of his age and had an ax put into his hand at once. And from that time to within his twenty-third year, he was almost constantly handling that useful instrument."

After all his toil and study, French was still not happy with the position of Lincoln's hands. The right hand did not seem natural. French's solution to the problem was to make a cast of his own right hand. One afternoon he went into the casting room of his studio, anointed his right hand, and had one of the studio workmen cast it in plaster. The next day he had the exact position he needed for the statue. The right hand was to hang over the arm of the chair, and a cast was made in that position. But the tapping finger still had its place. That's the exact position photographer Mathew Brady (1823–1896) caught when Lincoln was in conversation with his generals. In the final version of the statue, one hand is open and the other closed—a brilliant decision involving design and human anatomy.

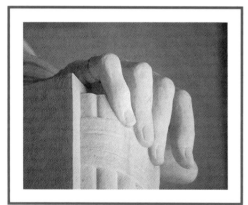

These are the hands Daniel Chester French sculpted for the Lincoln Memorial statue.

▲ Notice how French made
◀ the legs of the statue,
above and top left, seem
to change position when
viewed from different
angles.

In the three different consecutive models French made before completing the statue, his changes in the position of the hands and legs revealed much. Look at the three models and determine some of the changes he made. Perhaps you will begin to understand why he made them.

In the first model, the fingers of Lincoln's right hand are clenched. The left hand forms a pronounced right angle over the arm of the chair. The fingers are vertical and the hand proper is horizontal. The feet seem relaxed, with a trace of motion in the curve of the legs. In the working model, the feet, now reversed, are both firmly on the ground, and the hands show conflict between tension and calm. This time, it is the right hand that falls gracefully on the chair; the left is now clenched in a fist. In the final model of October 31, 1916, the tapping index finger on the right hand shows tension, while the left hand shows determination. The feet, solidly planted on the plinth, or surface above the pedestal, are firm and secure. Lincoln's hands and feet form a pattern. The legs balance the hands and arms.

three

Abraham Lincoln,
photographed by
Alexander Gardner
in 1865

In 1922, a month before the dedication of the Lincoln Memorial, an anonymous sculptor published an article with the following observation: "There are sculptors of the very highest rank who have declared it to be their opinion that, in spite of the greatness of the subject, in spite of the nobility of his achievements, in spite of the inspiration to be awakened by the contemplation of his extraordinary life, Abraham Lincoln is not a proper theme for sculptural treatment." The writer did not think that the man Lincoln had the look of dignity and beauty demanded of a monumental work of art. This statement may tell more about the state of sculpture in the United States than it tells about Lincoln.

In truth, America had no tradition in sculpture. Besides the carvings of the Native Americans, sculpture in the United States started with the old-fashioned whittling of Yankee farmers and stonecutters. In order to create masterful sculpture, an artist has to be able to see what other sculptors have done. Americans simply did not often have that opportunity. The sculpture that existed in the museums of Europe could not be reproduced like paintings could.

The American lack of appreciation for sculpture can be best illustrated by the experience of the English novelist William Makepeace Thackeray (1811–1863). Thackeray had come to the United States for a series of lectures on literature and art.

He noted that opposite the White House in Washington, D.C., there was an equestrian statue of General Andrew Jackson by a self-taught American artist of "no inconsiderable genius and skill." It happened that a member of Congress spoke to Thackeray about the work and asked, "Is it not the finest statue in the world?" Thackeray was bound to reply in a negative manner. Thackeray, who was somewhat of an artist himself, had a vast knowledge of European sculpture. "But you must remember," the congressman insisted, "that Mr. Mills had never seen a statue when he made this." So Thackeray suggested that "to see other statues might do Mr. Mills no harm."

Until the late nineteenth century, Americans had produced modest sculptures, but no world-famous sculptor had emerged. In the 1820s, American sculptors began to travel to Italy, where they were greatly influenced by the classical works they saw. Horatio Greenough (1800–1852) made one attempt at monumental sculpture. In 1832, many decades before French's *Lincoln*, Greenough went to Italy, where he sculpted the monumental *Statue of George Washington*. But Americans could not relate to its design. His *Statue of George Washington* was a modern version of the *Great Seated Zeus* by the Greek sculptor Phidias (430–490 B.C.). No American sculptor had dared to try anything of such monumental proportions. The sculpture was 10½ feet high and weighed 20 tons.

Greenough mounted Washington on a marble throne, cast drapery over his legs, and put sandals on his feet. The American public of the 1840s was outraged. One critic wrote: "Washington was too prudent and careful of his health to expose himself in a climate as ours, to say nothing of the indecency of such an exposure, a subject on which he was exceedingly careful." The lighting, too, in the original location of the sculpture, was a complete failure. To this day, Greenough's statue gathers dust in a dim alcove at the Smithsonian Institution in Washington, D.C. In sharp contrast, the statues of Lincoln by Daniel Chester French and Augustus Saint-Gaudens captured the character of Lincoln and the spirit of the American people.

When considering sculptures of Lincoln by American artists, the work of two other sculptors must be considered in addition to the French and the Saint-Gaudens sculptures. Though not well known, Thleda (dates unknown), a Native American artist, and Edmonia Lewis (1843–c.1900), an artist who was half African American and half Native American, add important statements to the history of Lincoln.

The Thleda *Lincoln* is a tribute to the man who indirectly saved a group of Indians from slavery and possible extermination. The Tlingit tribe lived mainly along the coast of southeastern Alaska. The Tlingits were divided into two groups—the Ravens and the Eagles. As the story goes,

▶ William Makepeace Thackeray, a nineteenth-century English author

▼ The nineteenth-century *Statue of George Washington,* sculpted by Horatio Greenough, is at the Smithsonian Institution in Washington, D. C.

This photograph is a copy of Thleda's Abraham Lincoln totem pole, originally carved and erected at Old Tongass Village.

a militant group of Eagles made war on a group of Ravens living on Tongass Island. For several years, the Ravens were driven from one refuge to another.

In 1867, the United States purchased Alaska from Russia. The following year the U.S. government established a customhouse and a fort on Tongass Island with a company of soldiers and a revenue cutter (a ship) assigned there to patrol the area and enforce law and order. When the Ravens, whose freedom was being threatened, learned about the nearby fort, they went there to seek protection. Government officials investigated the situation. The officials made it known to both the Eagles and the Ravens that under the new U.S. flag that flew over Alaska, slavery was illegal. They explained that Abraham Lincoln had freed all slaves in the United States and in U.S. territories. In appreciation of this protection, Chief Ebbetts, the leader of the Ravens, decided to erect a new totem pole to honor the great man

Abraham Lincoln, a bust sculpted by Edmonia Lewis

who had saved his people from slavery. An artist named Thleda, from the neighboring Tsimshian tribe, was hired to do the carving. Thleda worked from a photograph of Lincoln. The totem pole, the highest in the village, was raised in the 1870s with a great feast called a potlatch.

Another interesting and perceptive portrait of Lincoln is the work of Edmonia Lewis. Lewis was born near Albany, New York, of a Chippewa Indian mother and a free black father. Orphaned early, she was reared in the tribal tradition of her mother. Later Lewis went to Oberlin College in Ohio, and then she spent several years studying in Boston, Massachusetts. In 1865 Lewis went to Rome, where she met fellow Americans, such as the sculptor Hiram Powers. Lewis started her career as a sculptor in Rome. When she returned to the United States in 1873, Lewis went to California, where she experienced a spirit of freedom of expression unique to the West.

Lewis's *John Brown* (1876) bears some resemblance to her *Abraham Lincoln* (1867). She portrays John Brown as a thoughtful, almost saintly figure in majestic repose. He looks like a kindly, venerable gentleman with a sweet disposition. He must have been Lewis's hero, because her bust of Brown is much more powerful and expressive than her bust of Lincoln.

The photo at the bottom left was taken by Alexander Hesler in 1860. The other photos are by Mathew Brady. The top left photo appears on the U.S. five-dollar bill.

Since Lincoln was the first president to live in the age of photography, there are hundreds of different photographs of him. Lincoln's photographers struggled with his portraits, because his facial expression could change so quickly, thus changing his whole appearance.

Some people considered the president to be ugly. William Howard Russell wrote that Lincoln had a "strange gaunt face and head, great thatch of wild Republican hair, the prodigious mouth, the flapping ears." This was a kindly description compared to Colonel Theodore Lyman's description. Lyman, who was from Boston, described Lincoln's appearance in a letter to his wife. He wrote, "He [Lincoln] is I think the ugli-est man I ever put my eyes on. There is also an expression of plebeian vulgarity on his face."

Ugliness, ill health, or unusual features repulse certain people. Starting at an early age, some people base human popularity on good health and an attractive appearance. Someone with an evil nature may thereby disguise it with good looks. Or, as is often the case, false assumptions over-rule sensible judgments. For example, some people assume that a fat person is jolly, while a skinny, thin-lipped person is mean. Artists often see beneath the surface, however. Art can sometimes help us to see the truth that lies beyond our natural prejudice. Art is never a frill. In fact, it can often provide insight into human behavior. Let's see what insight the art of photography can reveal about Daniel Chester French's *Abraham Lincoln.*

Lincoln's looks were so controversial that the managers of his presidential campaign hired photographers to go to Springfield to take some "clean" pictures to distribute to the Eastern press. The photographs of Mathew Brady and Alexander Hesler are the most famous. Some historians credit the Brady photographs for the Lincoln victory of 1860 (in much the same way that TV makeup helped young John Kennedy win victory over Richard Nixon one hundred years later). Mathew Brady elevated portraiture in photography to an art form. His photographs are penetrating, telling, and even visionary.

▼ An 1860 presidential campaign poster shows a young Abe Lincoln with his running mate, Hannibal Hamlin of Maine.

▲ Abraham Lincoln in 1857,
photographed by
Alexander Hesler

On December 13, 1862, during Lincoln's second year as president, the Union suffered nearly 13,000 casualties at the Battle of Fredericksburg during the Civil War.

Photographer Mathew Brady

According to historian David Herbert Donald, Alexander Hesler's "sharply defined prints gave, as Lincoln said, 'a very fair representation of my homely face.' [The photographs] showed Lincoln at the height of his powers and captured, as no other photographs ever did, the peculiar curve of his lower lip, the mole on his right cheek, and the distinctive way he held his head. But most photographers found it hard to take a good picture of the candidate whose face in repose showed such harsh lines that it looked like a mask."

But Mathew Brady's photographs go beneath the public mask of the great president. In Brady's work, Lincoln's face becomes a window of his soul and inner turmoil. Since they were close friends, Lincoln was able to relax, and Brady was able to catch different aspects of Lincoln that reveal much. Brady used the lines of Lincoln's face, his eyes, and the position of his body to tell us about the man. In some ways, there is almost a sculptural aspect to Brady's photographs, especially in the hands and feet.

When you mount the steps of the Lincoln Memorial, you get a frontal view of the sculpture. The face reveals anger, anguish, and intense emotion. What is Lincoln thinking about? The answer is on the wall. The memorial is dedicated to two of Lincoln's speeches—the Gettysburg Address and the Second Inaugural Address.

No American president, no presidential speech writer, and few writers have come close to the rich texture of Lincoln's prose. Soon after the death of his own son and the slaughter of the young boys in war, Lincoln started to read the prophets of the Old Testament and the poetry of Robert Browning. Who does not thrill to the marching rhythms of Lincoln's prose or his prophetic style? Who is not inspired by his words?

"With malice toward none; with charity for all . . . "

" . . . that government of the people, by the people, for the people, shall not perish from the earth."

His words gave new meaning and the Lincoln stamp to the noble experiment—our American democracy. The Gettysburg Address and the Second Inaugural Address, in their essence, are the same speech. In their tone, however, they are quite different. The Second Inaugural has the voice of the angry prophet Isaiah: "Fondly do we hope, fervently do we pray, that this mighty scourge of war may speedily pass away. Yet, if God wills that it continue until all the wealth piled by the bondman's two hundred and fifty years of unrequited toil shall be sunk, and until every drop of blood drawn with the lash shall be paid with another drawn with the sword, as was said three thousand years ago, so still it must be said, 'The judgments of the Lord are true and righteous altogether.'"

Something wonderful happens as you move around French's statue of Lincoln.

The Second Inaugural Address

Fellow countrymen:

At this second appearing to take the oath of the presidential office there is less occasion for an extended address than there was at the first. Then a statement somewhat in detail of a course to be pursued seemed fitting and proper. Now, at the expiration of four years, during which public declarations have been constantly called forth on every point and phase of the great contest which still absorbs the attention and engrosses the energies of the nation, little that is new could be presented. The progress of our arms, upon which all else chiefly depends, is as well known to the public as to myself, and it is, I trust, reasonably satisfactory and encouraging to all. With high hope for the future, no prediction in regard to it is ventured.

On the occasion corresponding to this four years ago all thoughts were anxiously directed to an impending civil war. All dreaded it, all sought to avert it. While the inaugural address was being delivered from this place, devoted altogether to saving the Union without war, insurgent agents were in the city seeking to destroy it without war—seeking to dissolve the Union and divide effects by negotiation. Both parties deprecated war, but one of them would make war rather than let the nation survive, and the other would accept war rather than let it perish, and the war came.

One eighth of the whole population was colored slaves, not distributed generally over the Union, but localized in the southern part of it. These slaves constituted a peculiar and powerful interest. All knew that this interest was somehow the cause of the war. To strengthen, perpetuate, and extend this interest was the object for which the insurgents would rend the Union even by war, while the Government claimed no right to do more than to restrict the territorial enlargement of it. Neither party expected for the war the magnitude or the duration which it has already attained. Neither anticipated that the cause of the conflict might cease with or even before the conflict itself should cease. Each looked for an easier triumph, and a result less fundamental and astounding. Both read the same Bible and pray to the same God, and each invokes His aid against the other. It may seem strange that any men should dare to ask a just God's assistance in wringing their bread from the sweat of other men's faces, but let us judge not, that we be not judged. The prayers of both could not be answered. That of neither has been answered fully. The Almighty has His own purposes. "Woe unto the world because of offenses; for it must needs be that offenses come, but woe to that man by whom the offense cometh." If we shall suppose that American slavery is one of those offenses which, in the providence of God, must needs come, but which, having continued through His appointed time, He now wills to remove, and that he gives to both North and South this terrible war as the woe due to those by whom the offense came, shall we discern therein any departure from those divine attributes which the believers in a living God always ascribe to Him? Fondly do we hope, fervently do we pray, that this mighty scourge of war may speedily pass away. Yet, if God wills that it continue until all the wealth piled by the bondman's two hundred and fifty years of unrequited toil shall be sunk, and until every drop of blood drawn with the lash shall be paid by another drawn with the sword, as said three thousand years ago, so still it must be said, "The judgments of the Lord are true and righteous altogether."

With malice toward none; with charity for all; with firmness in the right as God gives us to see the right, let us strive on to finish the work we are in; to bind up the nation's wounds; to care for him who shall have borne the battle, and for his widow, and his orphan—to do all which may achieve and cherish a just, and a lasting peace, among ourselves, and with all nations.

▶ President Abraham Lincoln delivering his Second Inaugural Address in 1865

▼ A young man reads the words of Lincoln's Second Inaugural, carved on a wall of the Lincoln Memorial.

As you look at the sculpture from the side, Lincoln's tone and demeanor change. A magical transformation in his appearance occurs, similar to the transformation in the real Lincoln's appearance and in the tone of his speeches. Sculpture is three-dimensional and is to be experienced from front to back and from side to side. As you move around the statue, notice how French used Lincoln's face to reveal emotion. From the side view, the corners of Lincoln's eyes and mouth have been softened. No longer is the president ablaze in fury and anger. The eyes and mouth reveal gentle compassion and kind sympathy. Remember the Gettysburg Address—and the young men who did not die in vain. The words on the wall remind us of the horrors of the Battle of Gettysburg and the comforting tenderness of Lincoln.

French sculpted Lincoln's face to reveal emotion. As the viewer looks at the face of the statue from different angles, Lincoln's expression seems to subtly change.

The Gettysburg Address

On November 19, 1863, President Abraham Lincoln delivered a short speech at the site of the Battle of Gettysburg in Pennsylvania. In the speech, which ranks among the best remembered in American history, Lincoln tried to explain the purpose of fighting the war.

Four score and seven years ago our fathers brought forth on this continent, a new nation, conceived in Liberty, and dedicated to the proposition that all men are created equal.

Now we are engaged in a great civil war, testing whether that nation, or any nation so conceived and so dedicated, can long endure. We are met on a great battlefield of that war. We have come to dedicate a portion of that field, as a final resting place for those who here gave their lives that that nation might live. It is altogether fitting and proper that we should do this.

But in a larger sense, we can not dedicate—we can not consecrate—we can not hallow—this ground. The brave men, living and dead, who struggled here, have consecrated it [the Gettysburg battlefield], far above our poor power to add or detract. The world will little note, nor long remember, what we say here, but it can never forget what they did here. It is for us the living, rather, to be dedicated here to the unfinished work which they who fought here have thus far so nobly advanced. It is rather for us to be here dedicated to the great task remaining before us—that from these honored dead we take increased devotion to that cause for which they gave the last full measure of devotion—that we here highly resolve that these dead shall not have died in vain—that this nation, under God, shall have a new birth of freedom—and that government of the people, by the people, for the people, shall not perish from the earth.

Perhaps the best way to appreciate French's *Lincoln* is to compare it to the work of Giovanni Manzu. Many consider Manzu to be the best Italian sculptor in the last hundred years. Like French, Manzu wanted to capture more than just the physical features of his subjects. Because of his talent, the Catholic Church commissioned Manzu to do the official bust of Pope John XXIII (1881–1963). The selection of Manzu caused great difficulties for many officials within the church. Manzu was a Communist. Although he was a Catholic by birth, he was very anti-clerical. His religion was one of resent-

ment and rejection of the church and those who worked within it. When Manzu was notified of his commission to do the bust of Pope John, he had to resolve his own mixed feelings. Even if he did not personally hate the man, John, Manzu still

▼ The Gettysburg Address is carved on a stone plaque in the Lincoln Memorial.

The bust of Pope John XXIII by Giovanni Manzu

what miracle had allowed him to come to the throne of St. Peter?

During their many conversations, the focus of the portrait became the personality rather than the physical features of Pope John; the question was, how best to express it? Manzu was puzzled, but the pope looked at him with such warmth and affection—his face soft with a smile of comprehension—that the sculptor was overcome and glanced down at the pontiff's hands. Then he heard Pope John say, "Yes, yes, of course you must do a portrait that satisfies you. You must follow your conscience all the way. This must come before all else."

Manzu responded, "Thank you for understanding the principles of my work and my life. Thank you for allowing me my measure of dignity. Thank you for being pope. We have waited for you a long time, so long no one ever expected it to happen in our lifetime."

The ruling on the final bust of Pope John was quite clear. All other busts were to be destroyed, and the one remaining would become the official sculpture. Manzu did six models, each showing

hated his position as pope. According to Manzu, any official of the church had to be corrupt, perhaps even depraved.

Manzu mentions his feelings in his notes, and what happened to him is one of the beautiful stories of our time. Manzu received an invitation to meet and talk with Pope John. The pope's features initially confirmed Manzu's suspicion—big peasant ears, a bulbous face, and a fat nose. But discussions with Pope John revealed the pontiff's humanity, humility, and religious purity. As Manzu began to understand the pope, he looked into his eyes for some sign that the words he spoke did not express what John really felt. The sculptor saw nothing, however, except a broad smile. Here was a man, he thought, who most certainly was born to be a priest—but

▶ The final seven-foot clay model that French used for the Lincoln Memorial

▼ A preliminary sketch shows Lincoln with his left arm resting on his knee.

some kind of insight into the pope. In 1961, Manzu completed the final bust. In that year, while in very poor health, Pope John had signed the greatest encyclical (papal letter) of his reign, perhaps of the twentieth century: *Pacem in Terris—Peace on Earth.*

In Manzu's final bust, we begin to approach the sweetness of the man John. This final bust portrays Pope John's solid respect for order and the authority of the church. It also portrays John's sunlit smile. When the spirit of the subject penetrated the vision of the artist, Manzu—like French—was able to complete his work. After French had intensely studied the Brady photographs, the many

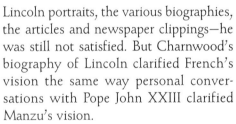

Daniel Chester French in his Chesterwood studio in 1925

Lincoln portraits, the various biographies, the articles and newspaper clippings—he was still not satisfied. But Charnwood's biography of Lincoln clarified French's vision the same way personal conversations with Pope John XXIII clarified Manzu's vision.

As a member of the Fine Arts Commission in Washington, French was closely associated with the plan for the Lincoln Memorial from its inception in 1911. French did not officially receive the commission for the statue of Lincoln until December 1914, however. Bacon and French decided that a statue must be the size demanded by the architecture, so the statue from head to foot is 19 feet high, the scale being such that if Lincoln stood up, he would stand 28 feet tall. It took many months of experimenting to decide on this size. French made several clay models of Lincoln, each time perfecting the details. Finally, he finished a seven-foot plaster model in his studio.

But there was still more work to be done, and on this French did not work alone. In his studio, he had photographs taken and blown up to approximate the final size of the monument. The statue still had to be carved in marble, and that work had to be done in a workshop. The

Pointing for enlarging a sculpture

▶ Most models for pointing are made of plaster, as was French's *Lincoln*. The locations of "points" are first marked on the model. In a large, complex work, these marks may number in the thousands. Several larger raised metal points in the model often serve as general locators for the pointing machine, which must be moved back and forth between model and carving many times before the work is complete. The final carving is often performed by the artist.

Pointing from plaster to marble

name for this carving process is *pointing,* and artisans who do it are called pointers. Pointing is a method of indirect carving—a mechanical process that exactly reproduces in stone a model that was conceived in another material, such as clay or plaster. Pointing is the process by which this transfer of image is accomplished.

The process of pointing still goes on in this country and around the world. Most sculptors are modelers who work in clay. Their work is then copied in marble or cast in bronze. For a time, critics noted the difference between clay modeling, carving, and pointing. Many artists and critics looked down on the pointing operation as

Pointing by compass in marble cutting

Daniel Chester French stands by as his *Lincoln* is assembled.

Getulio Piccirilli, the man on the ladder, is attending to an area on the marble where a hoisting handle had been.

merely a skill rather than an art form, but this assessment is not accurate. Pointing is a science and an art form. Pointing is a method of measuring, working by machine, and copying from one medium to another. The stonecutter's art is just as demanding as the sculptor's. Both need to visualize the final outcome. Without a talent for visualization, the stonecutter would be incapable of pointing and cutting marble. The Piccirillis were America's leading stonecutters for over 50 years.

Their contribution to America's monuments and statues is enormous. French insisted that only the Piccirillis were capable of pointing his statue.

The Piccirillis had a long tradition of sculpture in Italy. When the six brothers and their father came to America, several of them became gifted sculptors. They also established one of the finest stone-cutting firms in the United States. After French completed the model of *Lincoln,* he gave it to the Piccirilli brothers. They followed his design and built the statue.

Because the statue was so large, it was impossible to quarry one block of marble from which to carve it. The Piccirilli brothers worked simultaneously on 28 blocks of marble. The team was so talented that they could work in relays, one following the other on the same piece of stone, with perfect results. The Piccirillis finished the carving on November 19, 1919—almost a year from the time they began. During that year, French frequently visited their workshop to add his own touches with hammer and chisel.

Because of the importance of *Lincoln's* face, French entrusted to the Piccirilli brothers not only the seven-foot model, but also a full-size plaster model of the head of the statue. By so doing, the head could be pointed into marble without enlargement—thereby diminishing the potential for any loss of facial expression. The body of the seven-foot model was approximately tripled in size in the marble. When the carving was finished, the marble blocks were shipped to the memorial and assembled there. The artisans' work was so precise that it is hard to find the seams in the statue. This feat is especially significant since the entire piece weighs between 125 and 150 tons and, with the pedestal, stands 30 feet tall.

When French finished the final carving in the Lincoln Memorial in 1920, he said, "It is now as technically perfect as I can make it." The following year he returned to Washington, D.C., to view the statue. This time when he mounted the steps to look at his statue, it had a strange and startling appearance. Something had gone terribly wrong. It had never looked like this in the studio or when it was assembled and given its final touches. *Lincoln's* face appeared flat and white and frightened. French had spent six years of his life with a single purpose, and now something was wrong with the statue. Sadly, French realized that it was the lighting.

Bacon had first planned a ceiling of glass but later decided to use translucent marble. That decision deprived the statue of the strong overhead light in which it was created. Moreover, the public entrance was wide enough that the viewer looked toward the statue from the sunlit doorway. The sun streamed in, reflecting off the polished marble floor, which lit the statue from below. The white marble staircase and the reflecting pool of water in front of the memorial added another upward glare. For a sculpture, light and lighting are central concerns. Since it would take an Act of Congress to raise more money for the Lincoln Memorial project, French had to

explain clearly what had happened. In 1922 he had photographs made showing the statue under its best and worst lighting conditions. In *Journey into Fame,* Margaret French Cresson explains her father's problem: "A statue, to be well shown, should be lighted from above so that the shadows fall under the eyebrows, under the nose, under the chin, and so on. And here, because the light from below was so much stronger than that from above, the effect is exactly the opposite."

Desperate to do something to counteract the problem before the dedication ceremony, French decided to treat the marble. He mounted a scaffold again and for days supervised the tinting of the stone. To strengthen the shadows, he put extra heavy color around the eyes, but nothing solved the problem.

On May 30, 1922, former president William Howard Taft, who was then still president of the Lincoln Memorial Commission, presented the memorial to President Warren G. Harding. In his dedication speech, Harding recognized the real significance of the new memorial. He said, "This memorial, matchless tribute that it is, is less for Abraham Lincoln than for those of us today, and for those who follow after." Following the president's speech, Dr. Robert R. Moton, president of Tuskegee Institute, spoke. Moton urged black people and white people to join together to complete the work that Abraham Lincoln had begun. In signing the Emancipation Proclamation, Moton said, Lincoln had "freed a nation as well as a race."

Even with imperfect lighting, French's statue *Abraham Lincoln* was cherished, not only by Americans, but by people from all over the world. French, however, continued his quest. After several more years, the

◀ Sculptor Daniel Chester French, *left,* and architect Henry Bacon, *right,* at the Lincoln Memorial

▼ This composite photo shows the statue *Lincoln* under its best and worst lighting conditions.

◀ Abraham Lincoln's son Robert Todd Lincoln was a guest of honor at the dedication of the Lincoln Memorial.

▼ President Warren G. Harding dedicated the Lincoln Memorial on May 30, 1922.

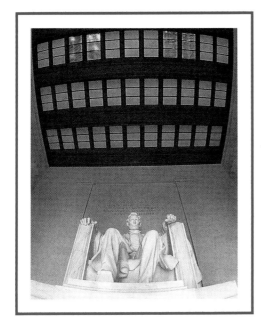

◀ The corrected overhead
▼ lighting, *left,* illuminates
the statue, *below,* as
French had intended.

problem was finally resolved in 1926, when artificial lighting was installed. The effect was extraordinary and satisfying.

French's monument is an important contribution to the history of American statuary and to the relationship between sculptor and architect. Daniel Chester French's *Abraham Lincoln* has become an American icon—an object of veneration. But it is more than that. It is a statue of the American soul, not only of what America is, but of what its people could be.

epilogue

◀ *Abraham Lincoln* seems to watch as Martin Luther King Jr. makes his famous speech during the March on Washington in 1963. His plea for justice and racial equality was a high point of the massive demonstration.

According to the Russian novelist Tolstoy, great art allows for the mingling of souls. In 1939, one of America's greatest contraltos, the African American singer Marian Anderson, had scheduled a concert at Constitution Hall in Washington, D.C. Racism had a strong effect on her career. Since she could not find work in the United States because she was black, Anderson had been singing in Europe. Due to racism, the Daughters of the American Revolution had her Constitution Hall performance canceled. But Eleanor Roosevelt would not hear of it. She stepped in and arranged for the concert to be held at the Lincoln Memorial.

▶ Martin Luther King speaking at the Lincoln Memorial

▼ Marian Anderson performing at the Lincoln Memorial

Anderson began her concert by singing "America." As that magnificent voice sang the words, "My country 'tis of thee," the souls of a hundred thousand people, joined by the music, mingled under the solitary gaze of French's *Lincoln*. Everyone now agrees that the proper stage for that con-

cert was the Lincoln Memorial, just as it has been for other significant events.

Standing in front of French's *Lincoln,* the statue of the Great Emancipator, Martin Luther King Jr. announced to the world that he had a dream of equal rights and dignity for all citizens. King called the Lincoln Memorial "this hallowed spot."

Many political monuments are massive, rhetorical, and boring. French's *Abraham Lincoln* is a political statement, but it is much more. It is sublime! His *Lincoln* was the best of his time—perhaps of all time.

Milestones in the Life of Daniel Chester French

1850 Born on April 20 in Exeter, New Hampshire

1860 Family moves to Cambridge, Massachusetts
Begins to show talent for carving

1867 Family moves to Concord, Massachusetts
Abigail May Alcott teaches Daniel how to model in clay

1870 Works in studio of John Quincy Adams Ward

1871 Studies anatomy with Dr. William Rimmer
Studies drawing with William Morris Hunt

1873 Awarded *Minute Man* commission

1874 Goes to Florence, Italy
Works in the studio of Thomas Ball

1876 Moves to Washington, D.C.
Begins first of three government commissions

1883 Commission to make the portrait statue *John Harvard*

1886 Travels to Paris

1887 Returns to United States

1888 Buys a house and builds a studio in New York
Marries his cousin Mary Adams French

1889 Commissioned to do *Milmore Memorial*
Daughter, Margaret, born on August 3

1891 Returns to Paris in November

1892 Commissioned to do *The Republic* for the Columbian Exposition in Chicago

1893 Columbian Exposition opens in May
Milmore Memorial, displayed in the Palace of the Fine Arts at the Columbian Exposition, receives international acclaim

1896 Buys Marshall Warner farm (Chesterwood), near Stockbridge, Massachusetts
Asks Henry Bacon to draw up remodeling plans

1900 Attends unveiling ceremony for *George Washington* in Paris with wife and daughter; travels to Greece and Rome
Elected to National Academy of Design
Begins work on *The Continents,* with Cass Gilbert
Elected trustee, Metropolitan Museum of Art
Melvin Memorial completed, with architect Henry Bacon
Appointed sculptor for the standing *Lincoln,* with Henry Bacon
Appointed member of National Commission of Fine Arts

1912 The standing *Lincoln* unveiled in Lincoln, Nebraska
Awarded the First Medal of Honor by the New York Architectural League

1913 Selected as sculptor for *Alger Memorial* in Detroit, with Henry Bacon
Commissioned for *Trask Memorial* in Saratoga Springs, New York, with Henry Bacon

1914 Offered commission as sculptor for *Abraham Lincoln* for the Lincoln Memorial

1916 Working model of *Abraham Lincoln* ready for inspection

1920 Finishes final carving of *Lincoln*
Sails for Italy

1921 Daughter, Margaret, is married

1922 President Warren Harding dedicates the Lincoln Memorial on May 30

1930 Created busts *Edgar Allan Poe, Phillips Brooks, Ralph Waldo Emerson,* and *Nathaniel Hawthorne* for the Hall of Fame at New York University
Appointed trustee of Saint-Gaudens Memorial in New Hampshire
Appointed trustee of Metropolitan Museum of Art in New York

1931 Daniel Chester French died in his cherished garden at Chesterwood on October 7.

1939 Mary Adams French dies.

glossary

architect: a person who designs buildings and other structures and oversees their construction

bondman: slave

commission: a formal, written authorization to perform a particular task; a group of people directed to perform some duty

emancipator: a person who frees others from bondage or slavery

horizontal: parallel to the horizon or to a base line

inaugural address: the speech the president gives after he takes the oath of office

intentional fallacy: an interpretation of a work of art based on the viewer's personal feelings

naturalistic: a realistic style that avoids idealization of a subject

oval: having the shape of an egg

plinth: the lowest part of a base

pointing: a method of indirect carving; a mechanical process that exactly produces in stone a model that was originally formed in another material

replica: a reproduction that is exact in all details

sculpt: to carve or model

sculptor: an artist who makes three-dimensional works of art, such as statues, by carving, modeling, or welding various materials

statuary: the art of making statues; a collection of statues

torso: a sculptured representation of the trunk of a human body—the body apart from the head, arms, and legs

vertical: upright

index

About the Author

Ernest Goldstein, a nationally acclaimed art educator and author, was born in Boston, Massachusetts. He attended the Boston Latin School and Brandeis University. After graduating in 1954, Goldstein received a French Government Fellowship and spent five years in France.

During the 1960s and 1970s, Goldstein combined two careers. He was a consultant to the Department of Health, Education, and Welfare's Bureau of Research, and he worked in publishing.

Both professions enabled him to visit classrooms and speak to students throughout the United States. His students ranged in age from preschool through graduate school. Because of his keen insights about art and people and his dramatic style of presentation, Goldstein kept his audiences, no matter what age, spellbound. His lectures have been described as "motivating, inspiring, instructive, and entertaining."

Some of Goldstein's other books include *Teaching Through Art, Understanding and Creating Art, The Journey of Diego Rivera,* and a series called Let's Get Lost in a Painting. Goldstein died in January 1996.

Acknowledgments

Don Berliner, 28 (all), 29, 45 (bottom left), 57 (bottom); Chesterwood, A National Trust Historic Site, Stockbridge, MA., 14, 50 & 52 (right) [Underwood & Underwood], 16 (lower right) [A.B. Bogart], 26 (both) [Michael Richman], 27 (both) [Bernie Cleff], 49, 55; Corbis-Bettmann, 9, 10 (bottom), 13, 17, 18, 36 (all), 39, 42 (both), 43; Erich Lessing/Art Resource, NY, 25 (both); Jack C. Rich. *The Materials and Methods of Sculpture.* Dover Publications, Inc., 1988, 51 (all); Jessie Tarbox Beals Collection, Francis Loeb Library, Harvard University Graduate School of Design, 11; Independent Picture Service, 40 (bottom); Library of Congress, 6, 10 (top), 20 (both), 23, 30, 31 (both), 38, 40 (top), 44 (top), 46, 54, 56 (top), 60 (left); Minneapolis Public Library and Information Center, 12 (top); National Archives, 52 (left); National Museum of American Art, Washington, D.C./Art Resource, NY, 16 (top left); National Portrait Gallery, Smithsonian Institution/Art Resource, NY, 21; National Portrait Gallery, Smithsonian Institution, 22; San Jose Public Library, 35; Scala/Art Resource, NY, 24 (all), 48; Skinner Auctioneers and Appraisers of Antiques and Fine Art, Boston and Bolton, Massachusetts, 49 (left); © John Skowronski, front cover, 2, 19, 44 (bottom), 45 (top left and right), 47, 57 (top), 62–63; Underwood & Underwood/Corbis-Bettmann, 56 (bottom); UPI/Corbis-Bettmann, 8, 12 (bottom), 58; U.S. Forest Service, 34; © Washington Post, reprinted by permission of the D.C. Public Library, 60 (right).